Glory

TO GOD IN

the highest

AND ON

Earth peace

GOOD WILL

toward

MEN

LUKE 2:14

Why Do We Celebrate Christmas?

Most of us know that Christmas isn't about the presents or the food or the days off of school or work.

We probably know that Christmas is about Jesus being born. But why is that a big deal, and how does that affect our lives more than the shiny gift with a bow under the tree?

There is so much "stuff" going on around Christmas, so sometimes it is hard to remember that God really really really loves us! And the reason Jesus was born as a baby and put in a manger and celebrated by shepherds and angels is that God wants to invite us to be His son or daughter, too!

You have a Heavenly Father who adores you and wants to speak to you. That's what Christmas is about!

How To Use This Bible Journal

I recommend that you start this journal the first week of December. For 4 weeks (5 days each week) you will focus on a couple verses in the Bible where Jesus tells us WHY He left Heaven and was born as a baby.

Each journal entry will ask you to:
　✷ **Take Notes**: jot down things you found interesting, definitions to words you don't quite understand, questions you have, etc.

　✷ **Key Scripture**: why did Jesus leave Heaven and come to dwell with us?

　✷ **Draw/Doodle**: explain the Scripture in a picture, what did you "see" while you read the verses?

　✷ **Prayer/Praise**: talk to God--ask for help, thank Him, etc.

　✷ **Note to Self**: what do you want to remember? how can you apply the Scriptures to your life?

BEHOLD
THE LAMB
OF GOD WHO
TAKES AWAY
THE SIN OF
THE WORLD
JOHN 1:29

week **1**

"And she will have a son, and you are to name him Jesus, for he will save his people from their sins."

Matthew 1:21

JESUS WAS BORN...
to rescue us from sin

NOTES:

KEY VERSE

DRAW/DOODLE

NOTE TO SELF

PRAYER/PRAISE

amen!

NOTES:

KEY VERSE

DRAW/DOODLE

NOTE TO SELF

PRAYER/PRAISE

amen!

Scripture:
Hebrews 2:14-18

Date:

NOTES:

KEY VERSE

DRAW/DOODLE

NOTE TO SELF

PRAYER/PRAISE

amen!

Scripture:

Romans 5:1-11

Date:

NOTES:

> **KEY VERSE**

DRAW/DOODLE

NOTE TO SELF

PRAYER/PRAISE

amen!

Scripture:
Luke 5:17-32

Date:

NOTES:

" KEY VERSE

DRAW/DOODLE

NOTE TO SELF

PRAYER/PRAISE

amen!

I AM THE WAY AND THE TRUTH AND THE LIFE NO ONE COMES TO THE FATHER EXCEPT THROUGH ME

JOHN 14:6

"But now God has shown us a way to be right with him without keeping the requirements of the law...."

Romans 3:21

JESUS WAS BORN...
to fulfill the Law for us

Scripture:
Matthew 5:17-18

Date:

NOTES:

KEY VERSE

DRAW/DOODLE

NOTE TO SELF

PRAYER/PRAISE

amen!

Scripture:
Galatians 3:10-4:7

Date:

NOTES:

> KEY VERSE

DRAW/DOODLE

NOTE TO SELF

PRAYER/PRAISE

amen!

Scripture:
Romans 8:1-4

Date:

NOTES:

> **KEY VERSE**

DRAW/DOODLE

NOTE TO SELF

PRAYER/PRAISE

amen!

Scripture:
Romans 10:1-13

Date:

NOTES:

> ❝
>
> **KEY VERSE**

DRAW/DOODLE

NOTE TO SELF

PRAYER/PRAISE

amen!

NOTES:

KEY VERSE

NOTE TO SELF

PRAYER/PRAISE

amen!

THE WORD BECAME

A HUMAN BEING

And Full Of

Grace & Truth

Lived Among Us

WE SAW
HIS GLORY

THE GLORY
WHICH HE

Received As

The Father's

Only Son

John 1:14

week
3

"Long ago God spoke many times and in many ways to our ancestors through the prophets. And now in these final days, he has spoken to us through his Son...."

Hebrews 1:1-2

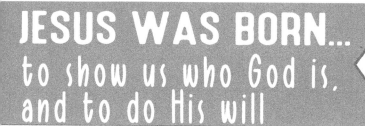

JESUS WAS BORN...
to show us who God is, and to do His will

NOTES:

KEY VERSE

DRAW/DOODLE

NOTE TO SELF

PRAYER/PRAISE

amen!

NOTES:

66

KEY VERSE

DRAW/DOODLE

NOTE TO SELF

PRAYER/PRAISE

amen!

Scripture:
Luke 4:16-21

Date:

NOTES:

KEY VERSE

DRAW/DOODLE

NOTE TO SELF

PRAYER/PRAISE

amen!

NOTES:

KEY VERSE

DRAW/DOODLE

NOTE TO SELF

PRAYER/PRAISE

amen!

NOTES:

KEY VERSE

DRAW/DOODLE

NOTE TO SELF

PRAYER/PRAISE

amen!

AND GOD SHOWED
HIS LOVE FOR US
By sending
HIS ONLY SON
Into The world
SO THAT WE
Might Have Life
THROUGH HIM
1 JOHN 4:9

"Though he was God, he did not think of equality with God as something to cling to. Instead, he gave up his divine privileges; he took the humble position of a slave and was born as a human being."

Philippians 2:6-7

JESUS WAS BORN...
as a humble servant

Scripture:
John 1:1-14

Date:

NOTES:

> ❝❝ KEY VERSE

DRAW/DOODLE

NOTE TO SELF

PRAYER/PRAISE

amen!

NOTES:

> **KEY VERSE**

DRAW/DOODLE

NOTE TO SELF

PRAYER/PRAISE

amen!

NOTES:

"

KEY VERSE

DRAW/DOODLE

NOTE TO SELF

PRAYER/PRAISE

amen!

Scripture:
Luke 2:1-20

Date:

NOTES:

> **KEY VERSE**

DRAW/DOODLE

NOTE TO SELF

PRAYER/PRAISE

amen!

NOTES:

DRAW/DOODLE

NOTE TO SELF

PRAYER/PRAISE

amen!

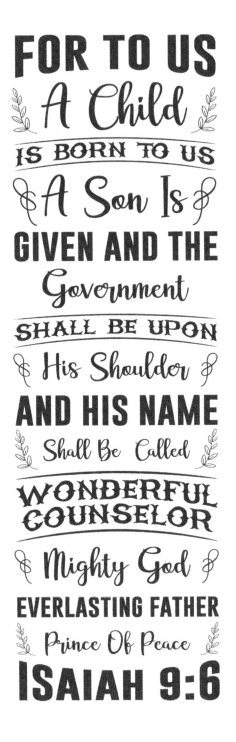

FOR TO US
A Child
IS BORN TO US
A Son Is
GIVEN AND THE
Government
SHALL BE UPON
His Shoulder
AND HIS NAME
Shall Be Called
WONDERFUL
COUNSELOR
Mighty God
EVERLASTING FATHER
Prince Of Peace
ISAIAH 9:6

Digging Into God Bible Journals are simple tools to inspire you to have your own special time with God.

If you are looking for something to help you, or your family, develop the joyful habit of spending time with the Lord each day, check out:

www.diggingintoGod.com

for Bible activity books, journals, and Bible studies for kids, teens, and adults.

Made in the USA
Monee, IL
10 December 2024

73088915R00030